NORTH POLE

Wally Herbert

For Kari

Contents

The North Pole

Of all the goals to which man aspired during the exploratory period of his time on earth, he chose as his supreme challenge to reach those two points about which the planet earth rotates. There, at those two desolate points, some 300 years after the first attempt, he finally set up the two greatest monuments that man the explorer ever erected on behalf of his country, his race, his creed, or as history will one day perhaps record it—in simple recognition of man's curiosity.

Those cairns of snow in point of fact were really rather small, but clearly what they lacked in size they gained through isolation, for they became at once the symbol of the vision and the noble courage of the heroes who had built them.

But the sequence of historical events which had led to these achievements did not end with the attainment of the Geographic Poles for it was very soon being vigorously proclaimed that a far greater challenge than reaching the Poles and returning along the outward route, was to cross the icecaps on foot. Such journeys, however, could not be made without the help of supporting parties or of aircraft in the case of the Arctic.

It is for this reason sometimes argued by those who have a passion for polar history but little or no experience of travelling in the polar regions that these achievements are hardly worthy of inclusion in the historical record along with those of the earlier attempts to reach the Poles unaided.

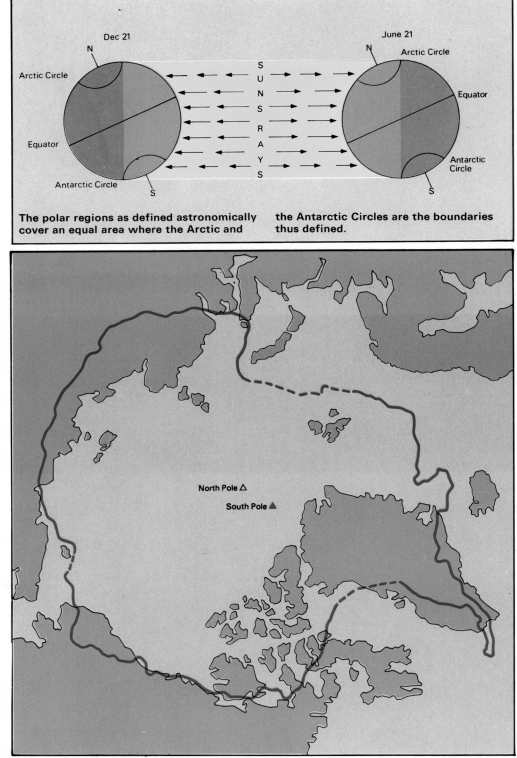

The polar regions as defined astronomically cover an equal area where the Arctic and the Antarctic Circles are the boundaries thus defined.

North Pole △
South Pole ▲

Above: In almost every other respect except for those phenomena related to light, magnetics and acoustics, the North and South polar regions are opposites. Similar though they are in size and shape with the Arctic Ocean and the Antarctic Continent each covering over 5,000,000 square miles, the one is an ice-covered ocean almost completely surrounded by land, the other is an ice-covered continent surrounded for most of the year by a frozen sea.

Left: The long polar night they have in common.

Above: Cold is also a condition of both— and although the Antarctic by virtue of its mass of ice is naturally the colder, a cup of boiling water thrown into the air when the air temperature is below −50°F (−45°C) will explode into a bursting cloud of minute ice crystals with equally dramatic effect in either Hemisphere.

Above: But it is on their differences that the polar explorer must concentrate his skills. Spectacular and hazardous though the Antarctic can be, the polar explorer is generally forced by the intense cold of winter to limit his period of travelling to the 100 days of summer when he has continuous daylight and is relatively warm.

Below: The Arctic Ocean on the other hand is covered by a skin of drifting ice which is

in a constant state of deformation as the winds and currents churn it around, fracturing it and pressuring it and grinding it into mush ice which will not bear the weight of a man. Across this the most variable and unstable physical feature on the face of the earth we planned to travel and drift for 16 months by a route from Alaska to Spitsbergen via the Pole of Inaccessibility and the North Geographic Pole.

The Search for the Pole

Curiosity was the one thing which all the early polar explorers had in common. Curiosity, however, was not motive enough to finance exploration and the course of polar history has therefore been influenced almost as much by the terms of its sponsors as it has by the explorers themselves. Queen Elizabeth I for example encouraged the merchants to sponser men such as Frobisher, Davis and Hudson to go in search of the elusive passage to the East.

But the quest for this route was often sidetracked by the discoveries that were made along the way, and the greatest of them from a purely commercial point of view was Hudson's discovery in 1607 that the waters off Spitsbergen were heaving with whales. He had set out with the intention of finding a short cut to the fabled riches of the East by sailing directly across the North Pole. Whaling, however, offered the sponsors a quicker return on their investment, and over the next 200 years became one of the biggest industries in the Western World. It brought fortunes to many and nations to the brink of war, and not until the beginning of the nineteenth century did a change of motive begin to affect the course of events.

The search for the North West Passage had by then become the proud prerogative of the Royal Navy, with the North Pole thrown in as a secondary objective. It took two more failures—Parry's attempt at the North Pole in 1827 and Franklin's at the North West Passage in 1845—before the race for the North Pole really began.

Above: Off the north coast of Spitsbergen in 1773, but for the intervention of fate, the destiny of a country might have changed, for the midshipman facing up to the polar bear is none other than Horatio Nelson.

Right: Parry's attempt at the Pole in 1827 was the swan song of a brilliant career for the drift of ice was against him.

Below: Kane's Expedition of 1853-5 opened up a new route to the Pole.

Bottom: The British made one last attempt at the North Pole in 1875–6 by methods already out of date, and finally lost interest when their hard-won record was beaten by the Greely Expedition in 1882 by a mere four miles.

Above: Henry Hudson—an explorer of great vision, but no match for a mutinous crew, was finally cast adrift in 1611.

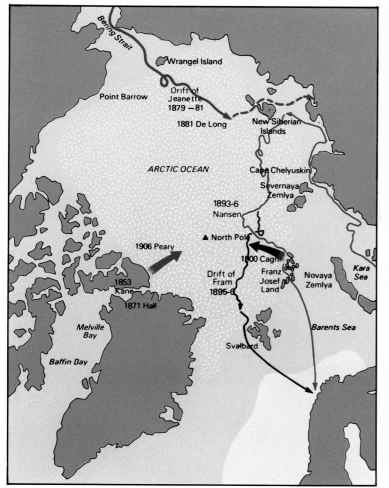

In 1879 George Washington De Long sailed the *Jeannette* into the Arctic Ocean through the Bering Strait and headed north hoping to make a landfall on the 'Continent' which he and many others at that time believed would be found in the higher latitudes. But his ship was beset, drifted for 16 months, and finally was crushed by the ice.

It was nevertheless the discovery of the wreckage of the *Jeannette* on the south-west coast of Greenland which inspired Fridtjof Nansen's theory that 'if a floe could drift right across the unknown region, that drift might be enlisted in the service of exploration'. He would build a ship that would withstand the pressure of the ice, provision it for several years, and drift across the Pole.

Admirable though his achievement was, however, his farthest north was still 226 nautical miles short of the magical 90° North and even before his book was published in 1897, Andree, a Swede, with two companions had made their ill-fated attempt by balloon.

All these attempts at the North Pole having failed, the time had finally arrived for the explorers to adopt the native techniques of travel and to employ the Eskimos to get them to the Pole.

Top left: The early attempts to reach the Pole.

Below: Nansen in one brilliant move advanced the whole concept of exploration by his epic drift in the *Fram*, for it was the perfect balance between science and adventure and conducted by a man of greater vision and adventurous drive than any other explorer the world has known. But even Nansen had become infected by the mood of excitement that had been spreading throughout the Western World over which national flag would be the first to fly at the Pole.

Top right: After the *Jeanette* was crushed by ice George Washington De Long and his crew had to abandon ship and try to journey across the ice.

Above right: For 33 years the fate of Andree and his two companions remained a mystery, but then by chance in 1930 the bodies and diaries of the men were found. They had crashed just short of the 83rd parallel, but having made their way safely back to land they died—probably of carbon-monoxide poisoning.

The Race for the Pole

Robert E. Peary was undoubtedly one of the toughest and most determined of men ever to direct his attentions towards the North Pole, and for his fanatical persistence if for nothing else he deserved the luck to reach it. But reaching it was not enough. Peary was obsessed by the need to be first. He saw the attainment of the Pole not only as his patriotic duty, but as the divine right of priority which had been promised *him*.

On his last and therefore most desperate bid to reach the Pole, Peary (who by then was 53 years of age) set out from Cape Columbia on 22 February 1909. His party consisted of 24 men, 19 sledges and 133 dogs. Strictly according to plan, one by one his 'divisions' turned back towards land having fulfilled their role as his stepping stones towards the Pole, until only Peary, his Negro manservant and four Eskimos remained.

On 6 April 1909 he claimed to have reached the North Pole, but a few days before he was able to send his triumphant message out to the world, a more dramatic announcement had been made by Dr Frederick Cook that he, accompanied by only two Eskimos, had reached the Pole on 21 April 1908—almost a year before Peary.

In order therefore to reap the rewards to which Peary believed he was entitled, he had first to discredit Cook, and this the Peary supporters did by a ruthless campaign of insults, slander, and the abuse of law and principle. Seldom in the short but dramatic history of the United States has a more vicious attack been made on the character and verbal integrity of one man in the interests not of truth but of the failed contender. The result was for Peary a tarnished prize, and for Cook the stigma and infamy of being labelled the world's most notorious liar—a label which (without any evidence to support it) discredits every historian who lacks the courage to challenge it.

Cook and Peary had hardly had time to shake the snow out of their beards before another explorer, Vilhjalmur Stefansson, came up with his theory that food to sustain both men and dogs could be secured anywhere on the Arctic Ocean.

Of the two claims to have reached the North Pole, there is no question to my mind that Peary's (above) is the weaker case. His only 'proof' that he reached the Pole are his recorded observations of the altitude of the sun; but these 'observations' anyone with a knowledge of navigational methods could have pre-computed in a matter of seconds.

Another criticism of Peary's claim concerns the distances that he covered during the unwitnessed stage of his journey. Even the average daily mileage he covered has never been equalled in a single day's march by anyone before or since and some of the distances he covered in the vicinity of the Pole are truly phenomenal.

Cook's claims on the other hand are perfectly feasible, and although his Pole computations were lost, his case is surely no weaker than Peary's on account of this, for his observations, like Peary's, would not in any case have proved that he had been there to anyone but himself. Of the two, the more remarkable journey without any doubt was Cook's, and there can be no further question that he made the journey he

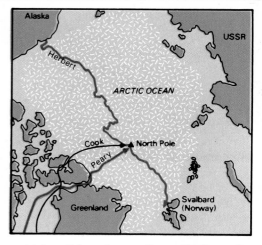

said he did as far as Cape Stallworthy and south to Devon Island, for I have followed every foot of his outward route and a good deal of his homeward march.

In summary then, neither claim can be proved nor can either claim be disproved and since there is not enough evidence to discredit either man it is unfair not to take them at their word.

But with the advent of aircraft, faster means of reaching the more inaccessible parts of the Arctic Ocean were soon at hand. This was demonstrated by Nobile and Amundsen in 1926 with the flight of the airship *Norge* (above left) from Spitsbergen to Alaska via the North Pole. This flight of 3,400 miles (5,470 km) took only 72 hours.

Then in 1937, the North Pole, after being the goal of so many expeditions, became the starting place for the drift of a Russian scientific station that had been flown in by aircraft. After a drift of eight months and over 2,000 miles (3,218 km) the team of four was picked up by icebreaker off the east coast of Greenland. This project was so successful that several other drifting stations, both Russian and American, were established after the Second World War.

From these drifting stations manned by scientists and technicians in relays over the years, the nature of the Arctic Ocean became a specialized study and the logistics operation of supporting them became a practised technique. By 1954 the commercial airlines were operating a fare-paying passenger service across the Arctic Ocean from Alaska to Scandinavia. Four years later the first submarine crossing of the ocean was made by the U.S.S. *Nautilus* (above right).

And so, on what grounds could anyone possibly argue the need for a journey by dog sledge across an environment as hostile as this when from any licensed travel agent one could buy an airline ticket across the top of the world?

'MAN HAS CROSSED ALL THE DESERTS, CLIMBED THE HIGHEST MOUNTAINS, MADE HIS FIRST CAUTIOUS PROBES INTO THE OCEANS AND INTO SPACE AND THERE IS ONLY ONE PIONEER JOURNEY LEFT TO BE MADE ON THE SURFACE OF THIS PLANET—
A JOURNEY ACROSS THE TOP OF THE WORLD.' (Wally Herbert, July 1967)

It was argued by many that such a journey was no longer necessary and that the risks were no longer justified. But I saw the Arctic Ocean as the setting for an epic trek across its longest axis—a journey of 3,800 miles (6,115 km) that would take 16 months to complete. Such a journey, historically speaking, would complete what man had only half accomplished with the attainment of the Pole. It would bring dramatically to an end the third and final human act in the trilogy of Mount Everest and the two 'super-mountains' at the top and bottom of the world.

But how were we to do it? The techniques of hauling heavy boats across the pack ice as Parry had done in 1827 and Nares had done in 1876 were clearly impractical. A surface crossing of the Arctic Ocean by Peary's system of supporting parties of Eskimos was not feasible because of the much greater distance we would have to cover. And Harrison's 1909 plan, by which over a period of two and a half years of continual travel he hoped to move in relays, a column of sixty sledges of vital provisions across the most unstable surface on earth, was clearly suicidal. Finally, there was Stefansson's theory that a good hunter could survive indefinitely on the Arctic Ocean. But of this I was not convinced for at no time during the 96 days in which Stefansson had put this theory to the test was he farther from land than 270 miles (435 km). What's more, there had been several occasions when, but for luck and a careful aim, he would have starved to death.

The Arctic Ocean at its longest axis could therefore be crossed, in my opinion, only by the carefully selective combination of the Eskimo techniques of travel and the most advanced form of logistics support—radios, homing beacons and satellite information on the weather and ice concentration. We, like Nansen, would make use of the drift, but unlike the *Fram*, which throughout its drift was imprisoned in the ice and had to go where it took him, we would be mobile. We would be the first scientific expedition to make a traverse of the Arctic Ocean by a route which we could adjust by physically moving our camp. But first we had to refine and test our equipment and techniques, and the best place to do this and learn something from the Eskimos was the Thule District of North-West Greenland.

11

The Polar Eskimos

No Eskimo community anywhere in the Arctic has been more closely associated with the attempts of the Europeans to reach the North Pole than the Polar Eskimos. This small and isolated tribe, whose first encounter with Europeans was their meeting with Ross and Parry in 1818, had believed themselves up till that time to be the only people on earth. And not without good reason, for there were no human beings to the north of them; none that they knew of to their west, and the treacherous ice of Melville Bay was in those days as much of a barrier to the south as the ice cap was to the east.

But exceedingly primitive though they appeared to the early explorers in this region, had it not been for the Eskimos, not a single man on Kane's expedition would have survived. The same can be said of Hall's. It is equally certain that Peary, Cook, Rasmussen and Koch could in no way have achieved their objectives without the loyalty and help of these proud hunters.

They put themselves at Peary's disposal partly in return for gifts; partly because he was a man of whom the Eskimos were far too afraid to flatly refuse; but mainly because they admired his courage and still do to this day. *Piularssuaq* they called him; he is a legend.

Nowhere in the Arctic is there to be found a greater variety of travelling conditions or any Eskimos more skilful in the art of driving dogs than in the Thule District. But tell that to three young men who had driven dogs more than 10,000 miles (16,093 km) in the Antarctic (which naively they believed was more difficult because it was unexplored) and they were due not only for a lesson in humility, but due also for a few shocks to their system and their preconceived opinions about the Eskimos themselves.

'These men, who have no fixed abode but live, as does their prey, ever on the move, are born Arctic explorers. From childhood they are hardened by an unmerciful cold, and their means of livelihood exposes them almost daily to severe physical strain and sudden dangers which sharpen their presence of mind and make their contempt of death a matter of course, the consequence being that they are unsurpassed as companions on Arctic Expeditions.'
(Knud Rasmussen, 1921)

Above: The old men naturally tend to take life at a slightly slower pace.

The Crucial Test

The winter we spent in the Thule District of North-West Greenland was the first part of our training programme. It was a period of preparation for the second part, a journey of 1,500 miles (2,414 km) which was to be the crucial test of our equipment and technique.

As for the choice of route, it was necessary to select one that would be every bit as punishing to ourselves and our equipment as the much longer journey across the Arctic Ocean. This requirement had left us with no alternative but to attempt the route taken by Dr Cook in 1908—a journey which, after the first month when we parted from the Eskimos, was to become a desperate struggle for survival. At times we were able to keep going only by feeding dog to dog and hauling the heavy sledges ourselves, and times when we were so weak that we could barely stand. But I had to learn, the weakness in our equipment, in the plan, in my companions and in myself. On a short pleasant journey we would have learnt nothing.

When we had completed the journey we at least knew that if we were to get the best out of our dogs and get half of them through to Spitsbergen we would need dog food enough to leave a trail of surplus food right the way across the Arctic Ocean. We would need supply drops to enable us to travel light; sledges based on the Eskimo design, but made of the finest seasoned oak and built by master craftsmen. We would need reserve sledges on hand at Point Barrow and Resolute Bay that could be flown out to us at short notice and reserve tents, sleeping bags, primus stoves, food—reserves of everything. Each sledge would have to be a self-contained unit down to the smallest item of gear. We would need lightweight, robust radios with a range of over 1,000 miles (16,093 km). We would need furs similar to those used by the Eskimos; but, most important of all, we would have to move like Eskimos and train ourselves in a crisis to think and behave like Eskimos.

Above: By the time the sun returned we were already nearing the end of our journey across Smith Sound with the Eskimos and about to begin the most terrible journey that we had ever experienced.

Left: The route of the Greenland Training Programme and the proposed route of the trans-Arctic journey.

Below left and right: The route taken across Ellesmere Island by Dr Cook in 1908 had been done only once before, by Otto Sverdrup, and only twice since. But from the accounts of these three crossings there had been snow on the route and none of them had been obliged, as we were, to go down into the canyon and travel its full length manhauling the sledges over frozen waterfalls and through places where the canyon was not even wide enough to get the sledges through without dismantling them.

Right: Towards the end of the journey the hunting improved, but by then we were in a desperate race to get to Resolute Bay before the break-up of the ice.

Above: Once through the canyon we had hoped our troubles would be over. But we still had a long way to go over stony ground and along frozen braided streams before we reached the sea ice on the west coast of the island, and by that time the only food left was the flesh of the dogs that were too weak to continue.

Right: We were now travelling for 14 hours a day and stopping for an occasional brew of tea—but we had learnt many lessons on this journey and swore never to repeat our mistakes.

Plans and Preparations

By the time I arrived back in London on 30 June 1967, less than six months were left in which to launch the main expedition. Although we had literary contracts that were expected to yield some £48,000, only £8,000 of this had been received and £7,000 had already been spent. That we finally raised sufficient funds, ordered and shipped 70,000 lb (31,750 kg) of equipment to the two staging depots in the Arctic, and transported 40 huskies from northwest Greenland to Barrow, Alaska, all within the space of a few frantic months, was as much a credit to our suppliers as it was to my small staff and the enthusiasm and encouragement of our Committee of Management

The logistics support, so vital to the Expedition, had been promised by the Canadian Forces and the Arctic Research Laboratory at Barrow. The Royal Air Force had flown all the expedition's equipment to the two Arctic staging depots. The hut in which we had spent the winter in Greenland had been flown to Resolute Bay, where it was to be stored until it was needed by us in the middle of the Arctic Ocean, and the Royal Navy had agreed to schedule HMS *Endurance* for standby duty in Spitsbergen waters to cover the closing stages of our journey in June 1969.

But the end of the journey still seemed a long way off when I left London for Alaska on 10 January 1968 to join Allan Gill and Ken Hedges, a doctor in the Royal Army Medical Corps who had taken the place sadly vacated at the end of the training journey by my old friend Roger Tufft. As far as the paperwork was concerned, however, that stage of the expedition was now over. The airdrops had been carefully scheduled and all the gear for each drop sorted and weighed. The direct radio link between Squadron-Leader Freddy Church, RAF, our radio relay officer at Barrow, and Cove Radio, The Royal Aircraft Establishment's experimental radio station at Farnborough, had been established, and the sledges and equipment had all been checked. We were insured even against failure to set out.

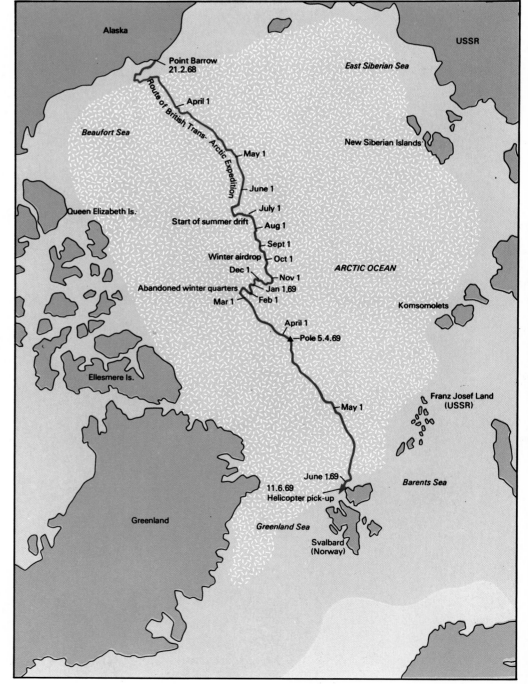

Naturally I was secretly worried about many things. Would the dogs last the distance? How well would we ourselves cope with the sheer monotony and the continual and crippling physical toil of a 16-months' journey? Hard though the training programme had been, at least we had had some variety in the scenery. There had been physical landmarks for which, on the trans-Arctic journey, I had to find a psychological substitute. Ahead lay a journey which no one before had ever attempted. It was a journey four times as long as the ordeal of the previous spring, and six times as long as an Antarctic sledging season. Besides breaking up the journey into five seasonal phases, I therefore deliberately broke up the diet so that with each change of phase we would have a change of food. I made provision for each man at all times to have his own team of dogs, with eight spare sledges held in reserve at Barrow and Resolute Bay. In this way each man would have a pride in his team and friction would be kept to a minimum. We would only meet up with each other during the day when we encountered some obstacle to our progress and would therefore look forward to the company of our tent companions at the end of each day's toil. For convenience I had adopted the time-honoured arrangement of two men to a tent, but had taken the precaution of arranging for a changeover of tent companions at the end of each 30-day period so that we could avoid the 'two-tent split' so common on Antarctic expeditions, where two partnerships of a four-man party are practically strangers to each other. But, most important of all, my arrangements for search and rescue, which had been worked out in considerable detail, I kept strictly between me and those who would operate the plan. My companions knew nothing about it (and surprisingly never asked) and were therefore able to concentrate their minds on the objective of getting across the Arctic Ocean safely.

Point Barrow

With Dr Fritz Koerner's arrival at Barrow on 8 February 1968 the Expedition was complete and ready to set off, for, in his absence, his team of dogs had been worked by one of the Eskimo employees of the Expedition's hosts, the Naval Arctic Research Laboratory. But to have set off then would have been suicidal. Over the last two weeks I had flown many times over the sea ice in the Laboratory's light aircraft looking for a route across the fractured young ice that drifts along that desolate coast. Each time I had returned dejected, for what I had seen on those reconnaissance flights was a belt of sea ice far more open and active than I had expected. There was no alternative but to wait at Barrow for the winds and currents to work in our favour and jam the young ice in the 80-mile (128-km) gap between the coast and the polar pack.

The date I had originally set for our departure had been 1 February. On that date at the latitude of Barrow there are barely four hours of twilight; but we had hoped by starting early to get to a position some 60 miles to the east of Barrow, and from there make a dash for the polar pack 80 miles to the north at the moment the ice ceased working. This moment we had hoped would come 48 hours after a storm had died, leaving us two or three days at the very most to reach the relative safety of the thicker floes before the next big blow. We had expected and were prepared for forced marches in darkness across thin ice and fields of pressure. We were keyed up, tense and eager to get this dangerous phase of the journey behind us. But we were totally unprepared for the strain of delays and the irritation of critical comment.

The pessimists predicted that we would get no farther than the mush ice belt and odds of four to one against us were being offered in the bars of Fairbanks. It came as a surprise to learn later that cash bets were still changing hands on whether we would give up before the summer even when we were more than 300 miles (482 km) out. The reason for doubt evidently was that we were using techniques of sledge travel regarded as obsolete by all but a few of the older Eskimos from

Barrow. We were wearing woollen clothing and furs in preference to the latest mode in polar clothing. We were using robust but low-powered radios against the advice of several Arctic radio experts, who could only think in terms of static stations where there was plenty of power at hand. And we were frowned upon by many adventurers for planning our logistics support on the assumption that we would see insufficient wildlife to sustain four men and four teams of dogs throughout the 16-month journey.

It was even said by one critic that in attempting to cross the Arctic Ocean by its longest axis we would benefit so greatly from the drift of ice that we would reduce the ordeal by 10 per cent and make a mockery of the challenge. We were therefore by some considered behind the times and, by others, unsporting.

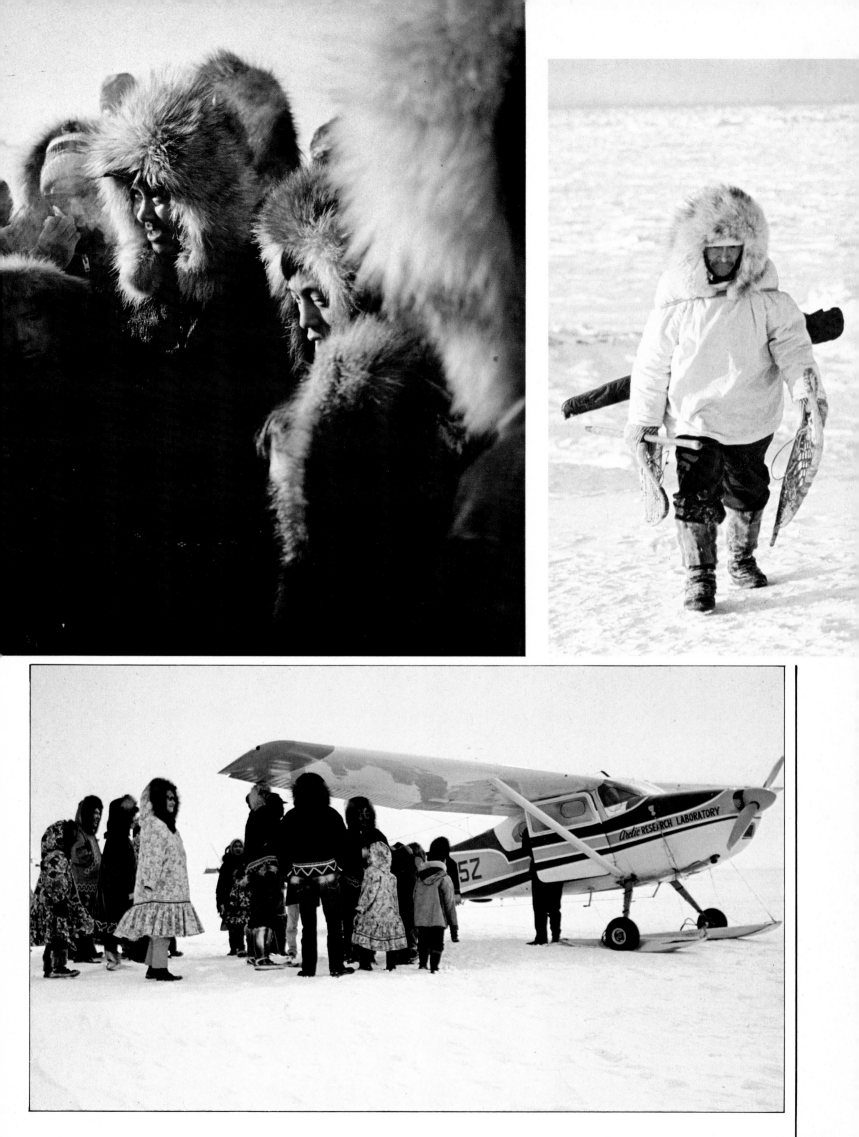

The Eve of Departure

For three weeks we waited. We listened to the Eskimos and sought the forecasts of weather experts. We watched the sun rise higher each day and saw bets changing hands between the cooks and laundrymen in their rare moments of speculation on our prospects of survival. We became a topic of conversation among the Eskimo community at Barrow. Most of it was prophetic, for the older ones had all heard stories about hunters who had met with some disaster on the drifting ice. A few even spoke from experience and advised us to give up the idea there and then—or at least to avoid the terrible 'whirlpool' known as Hell's Hole. It was said to exist about 200 miles (322 km) to the north of Barrow, although nobody was quite sure. We were also told folk tales by the score and one which to this day I recall was about an Eskimo hunter from Barrow (many, many years ago) who travelled alone across the polar pack ice to a place where he discovered people who were, it is said, very strange to behold. But they were evidently a friendly tribe and realising that no one would believe his story when he returned to Barrow, they obligingly tattooed a whale on his back.

During the last few days before setting out, however, we came under a new and more sinister strain. Press agencies, puzzled by our delayed departure, were becoming suspicious and it was evident from the number of telephone calls from the news media in London and New York that they had caught scent of a potential disaster and would be satisfied with nothing less.

Below: The Naval Arctic Research Laboratory from the air.

The expedition had taken four years to plan from the first seed of the idea to the eve of departure. To the north, not 200 yards away, was the Arctic Ocean, its surface as unstable and perhaps as unsafe as any area on earth. Our proposed journey along the longest axis would be a pioneer journey. It would be a horizontal Everest that would dig so deeply into our reserves of courage that it would mark each one of us for life. Our beds, some nights, would be on ice that was no more than a few feet thick and would sometimes be very much thinner. It might split or start to buckle under tremendous pressure at any time. There would not be a day during the next 16 months when the floes over which we were travelling, or sleeping off our fatigue, would not be drifting with the currents or being driven by the winds. There would be no end to the movement; no rest, no landfalls, no sense of achievement, no peace of mind, until we reached Spitsbergen.

'By midnight on the eve of our departure the pace of preparations had slackened. It was like the eve of a battle—still, clear, cold, silent, with no one sleeping; an atmosphere heavy with

private thoughts. I had been through these last quiet hours so many times before in my long polar career, but somehow this was different. Alone in the warehouse, loading my sledge, I found myself thinking of the struggles and hard times of the last few years, the crises, the frustrations; and how, but for the faith of my parents and a few close friends and the encouragement of my committee and colleagues, this dream with which I had lived for so long could never have become a reality. The expedition for me was already half over; for Allan, Fritz and Ken, it was about to begin.'

Setting out from Barrow

Over at the rocket launching site the road ended and the trackless waste began. It had been decided therefore that that would be the practical if not the most appropriate place for the well-wishers to gather and by midday a sizeable crowd had made their way there from the Naval Arctic Research Laboratory and the Eskimo village of Barrow in relays of truck loads and private vehicles.

They were a motley collection, perhaps about 200 in all. Most of them were wearing khaki parkas with enormous fur-lined hoods. Some had their hands in their pockets, others were gently pumping their arms to keep themselves warm. But none of them spoke, and when we moved away they were still there, standing silently as they had stood on our arrival, until they were lost in the trail of vapour left behind by our panting dogs. I turned away and looked east. The wind bit into my face. I pulled the hood of the wolfskin parka across my line of vision and huddled deeply into a protective shell of fur. The date was 21 February 1968 and the longest sustained sledging journey in the history of polar exploration had finally begun.

Never in my life had I been more afraid or more in awe of my own

ambition than when I saw it for the first time in proportion to the challenge it had chosen to accept, and I cursed wih all my heart the stubborn pride and folly that had led me to that place. But what of my companions who were following my tracks? Could I admit to them the fear that I had overreached myself and overestimated even their ability to cope? Perhaps they were as scared as me and all of us were

grasping at the others for support without openly admitting that we needed any help. In that case we would all four go together to our death and our folly would be news one day and forgotten by the next.

But for how long these thoughts plagued my mind I cannot now recall. Perhaps they lasted only seconds—perhaps for 16 months. All I know is that without this fear the challenge has no cutting edge.

We needed these fears to stimulate the will to overcome them, and we need to keep them secret, for the fear expressed is never lessened by the act of sharing.

Left: The first priority was to locate the smooth stretch of ice that I had seen on the last reconnaissance flight, for it was only by this route that we could quickly reach the point some 60 miles (96 km) to the east of Barrow from which we might make a dash across the 80-mile (128-km) wide stretch of fractured young ice which separated us from the polar pack.

Above: It was not certain that the route we had seen from the air would hold together, but the omens were good—it was still calm and the air temperature was steady on −40°F (−40°C).

Right: When we reached that point on 25 February, however, everything had changed. From the top of a wall of pressured ice all we could see was chaos and no way seemed humanly possible except the route by which we had come.

Camps Adrift

'The alarm would wake us at six o'clock and the man whose turn it was to make breakfast would ease himself out of a frozen shell of warmth and fumble in the dark for a match. A sharp scratch, a spurt of light, and a flame would grow at the end of a stick that would snuff itself out as it reached the lamp and moved under the glass towards the wick. At the second or third attempt it would catch and the tent fill with yellow light. A burning match would light the fuel in the priming cup of the kerosene stove, then the cook would shrink back into his bag.

'Hoar frost and ice glazed the head of the bag and coated the walls like fungus. Hoar frost like fleecy beards hung from the clothing in the apex of the tent, and trembled as breath vapour floating in curls drifted up among them on a rising draught of warmth. A leg, stiffened with morning cramp, would shake loose a cascade of delicate crystals that would float down on the two men and settle like spiders' webs on the face of the one who was watching the priming fuel licking the burner tubes of a grimy stove.

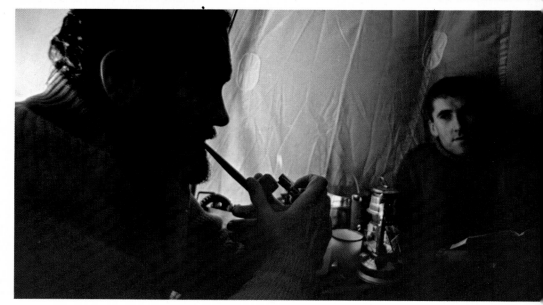

'He would release two arms from the warmth of the bag and with grubby hands wipe the melting hoar frost evenly over his face and poke his fingers into his ears. His morning ablutions done, he would pump the stove, which would splutter and fire. The pot, which the night before had been filled with water and which now was frozen solid, he would place on the stove, and while the flame cupped the pot like a blue-fingered hand and the ice contracted with pings and cracks, the cook would wriggle once more into his cozy cocoon.

'Few words were passed at that time of the day, for not until the stove had been burning for half an hour would the temperature in the tent have risen from −45°F (−42°C) to a tolerable −35°F (−37°C). We started each day with a cup of tea and followed it with porridge, with as much butter as we could afford chipped off its frozen block and buried in the simmering goo. Sugar and milk were added, and at this stage in the journey we would even have a second course of bacon and biscuits. Two more cups of tea would complete the meal and we would pack up and go. The walls of the tent by then were wet, and the clothing that had been hanging in the apex overnight limp and damp.

'We moved around outside with lamps and fumbled through the twilight, breaking camp and loading the sledges, untangling the dogs and hitching them up; and by 8 am with our wolfskins frozen as solid as suits of armour, we were on the move, cutting through the cold, with each footstep jarring the body back to the misery from which it had been released by sleep only seven or eight hours before.' *(Across The Top of The World,* Wally Herbert*)*.

ITEM	oz.	kcal
Butter	4.5	1012
Meat	6.0	972
Chocolate	4.0	656
Sugar	4.2	470
Milk powder	2.0	300
Cheese	1.0	142
Biscuits	4.0	556
Oats	2.4	307
Sweets	0.5	45
Drinking Chocolate	1.5	192
Potato powder	1.0	156
Glucose lemon	1.0	112
Soup powder	1.0	100
Fruit bar	0.75	52
Coffee (Nescafe)	0.25	6
Pumpernickel	—	—
Tea (leaves)	0.25	—
Curry powder	0.25	—
Salt	0.4	—
Onion flakes	0.4	—
Vegetable extract	0.1	—
Egg powder	0.4	62 (?)
Bacon	1.6	200 (?)
Jam	0.1	10 (?)
TOTALS:	37.6	5350 (min)

The most significant difference in the rations of the old explorers compared against the modern sledging ration is in the balance of the main items and in the fuel consumption. The food carried by the old explorers (with the exception of Mikkelsen) was more in weight per man/day than the proposed ration for the British Trans-Arctic Expedition, and yet in caloric value the B.T.A.E. ration was higher. (Captain Scott manhauled on 4,068 Kcal/day as compared with the minimum of 5,350 Kcal/day British Trans-Arctic ration.)

The fuel carried on modern expeditions is almost twice as much as during the 'heroic age' although the total weight of food and fuel is comparable.

The Dogs

Every item of equipment that was being used on the journey across the Arctic Ocean had been designed by man to serve a need or perform a specific function. The dogs on the other hand had neither been created by man nor put on earth, as far as we know, specifically to serve him. How then could we justify using dogs on a journey such as this—a journey on which there was no guarantee that any of them would survive? To answer this question of conscience and to understand the relationship which exists between the Eskimo (or the explorer) and his team of dogs, one must look at the basis of mutual trust upon which this relationship was built several thousands of years ago.

As a primitive hunter, man lacked mobility; the wild dog lacked the foresight and the ingenuity of the human being—and so they united and became as partners supreme among all the predators on land, and as friends more loyal than any other partnership known to the animal kingdom.

What the dog requires from this partnership as far as one is able to judge is really very little. In a pet this probably amounts to no more than ample food and affection. But the sledge dog needs two more things from its master: it needs discipline and encouragement. Within the team, the dogs establish for themselves an order of rank of which the king dog is the head. This 'pecking order' is constantly changing and even the king dog from time to time will have his authority challenged. The one stabilizing factor in the team—the one constant source of authority—is the man who feeds and drives them. It was for this reason (among others) that I decided we should each have a team and keep to the same team throughout the 16-month journey.

The advantages of dogs over machines are of course decreasing as the machines become more reliable, and already by 1968 the snow-mobiles had replaced the dogs in all but a few of the most isolated and traditional Eskimo villages because the machines were faster and did not require fuel or any attention (so the less mechanically-minded Eskimos thought) when they were not being used.

On a journey such as ours, however, the dogs were not only more reliable, but absolutely essential. If one vital part of a machine is broken and cannot be replaced, the machine is of no more use except as an immobile set of 'spare parts' for the machines that are still working. If on the other hand one dog dies, the team has lost only one-tenth of its power and after feeding, so to speak, upon a part of itself, it can continue and even increase its range by consuming the 'fuel' that the missing part would otherwise have used. In addition to this, the dogs are more versatile than the machine—they can jump across fractures in the ice and swim if they fall in; they can warn the sleeping drivers of the approach of a bear and feed upon its carcass; they can be refreshed by resting and, if the journey is long enough, they can procreate themselves. Last but not least, they are themselves a source of food when no other hope of survival exists for the explorer whose radio has broken down way out in the middle of the drifting polar pack.

— Of the 40 dogs that started out from Alaska, only four failed to complete the 3,720-mile (5,986 km) journey, and of those four, three were lost within the first week.
— The youngest was about 2 years, the oldest about 5 years.
— The average weight was about 90 lbs (41 kg) and they could haul at least twice their own weight for eight hours a day under normal pack ice conditions.
— They were fed $1\frac{1}{2}$ lb of pemmican a day and for water they ate snow.

The dog's harness these days is made from tubular nylon webbing, which has the advantage over sealskin of being less appetizing, more supple, and easier to sew. Each harness must be tailored to fit the dog perfectly, so that the full weight of the pull is taken against the chest.

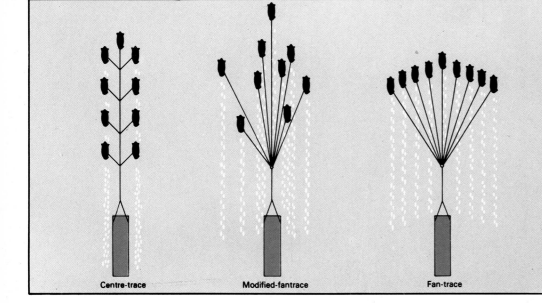

Centre-trace   Modified-fantrace   Fan-trace

Each of the three trace systems illustrated has its pros and cons. With the centre trace system the dogs tend to pull harder and more consistently, but the system lacks flexibility. With the modified fan the dogs can spread out or bunch up depending on the surface, but it is an awkward compromise between the centre-trace system and the fan trace, the last of which is without question the most natural formation for a pack of dogs and the one which the dogs clearly prefer. The 'pure' fan is also the one which requires the greatest skill on the part of the driver and offers the greatest variety of sledging techniques. This is the system used by the Polar Eskimos, and the one which in all but the roughest ice conditions was used by us.

The Mush Ice Belt

By the end of the first week we had reached a point about 75 miles ENE of Barrow and were still on the south (and safe) side of the mush ice belt and still looking for a suitable place at which to cross it. Up till then, although the going had been hard, we had at no time been in any danger. But on the evening of the ninth day out, any hope of an easy way onto the polar pack was shattered.

'It was a beautiful evening; a dead calm evening; the temperature was minus forty Fahrenheit. The rattle of pots and pans and the roaring of the primus stoves from the two tents was a soothing sound. Outside, Fritz and I were doing a few last chores, and the dogs were scratching nests for themselves out of the hard-packed snow and circling in a spiral, their noses pursuing their tails as they curled into tired balls and sank. The sun was still catching the tents and tinting the steam which poured from the vents as Fritz, his chores done, crawled through the sleeve entrance into his tent. I could hear him chatting with Allan as I stretched out the radio aerial, found a dog in the way, and eased him out of his nest with the toe of my boot. I heard a soft growl—then four or five sounds like pistol shots.

'It was as though several unseen blades had slashed the ice in a movement quicker than the eye could catch; six parallel cuts, two on one side, four on the other, leaving the tents on a strip of ice no wider than twenty yards. Within seconds the splits had opened a couple of feet, and by the time the others were out of the tents the fractures were over a yard wide and fog-like clouds of frost smoke were beginning to rise from the water.

'We hurriedly broke camp, but just as we were lashing up the sledges, the narrow strip of ice on which we were standing cracked at right angles to the first fractures, reducing the area in which we could manoeuvre the dogs and sledges to a rectangular pan of ice about sixty feet by eighty. There was no escape route east, west or south, for in those directions the floe had completely shattered. In the fading light the pans of ice appeared to be spreading out and

slowly gyrating. Our only chance was the small hummocked floe to our north—a heavy-looking mass of ice with a profile so jagged that we were not too sure we would be able to get onto it. We persuaded the dogs by the whip to leap the first open fracture without difficulty, but had trouble getting them over the second—a seven-foot gap. Those that hesitated we had no alternative but to pick up and throw bodily into the cold black water and force them to swim across to the other side. The sledges all dipped their rear ends into the sea, but by beating the dogs and keeping them moving the sledges rode out. By the time we had pitched camp about a hundred yards onto the floe, the night was pitch dark.'

'We slept fully clothed and kept watches for the rest of that night (a routine which became essential in our fight to survive during the next sixteen days), and as dawn approached, not two hundred yards to our north, where earlier I had seen a narrow belt of mush ice, there was now a vast area of "smoking water".'

The Throat of Death

It must have looked a precarious spot to Bob Murphy when he flew over us on the morning of 1 March in one of the Naval Arctic Research Laboratory's Cessnas, and what we suspected he later confirmed by radio: we were still about 40 miles (64 km) south of the polar pack ice edge and the whole area between the coast and the polar pack was breaking up. But the other piece of information he passed on to us came as a complete surprise: in the last 48 hours we had been carried by the drifting ice 15 miles (24 km) to the west.

We broke camp immediately and sledged due east and by late afternoon we had covered 2 miles (3 km) and reached a flat stretch of ice which had, that morning, been projecting like a prominent cape into the sea of open water to our north. The floes that had been on the northern horizon that morning had meanwhile closed in, and were moving at about three knots past the floe on which we were standing and at the point where they were making contact a huge ridge of ice was building. Great slabs of ice were creeping up the sides of a 20 ft (6 m) moving wall, from the inside of which were coming the most terrible sounds of groaning and screeching. Blocks of ice, some of them no doubt weighing several tons, were falling from it as it advanced, but its rate of movement and direction seemed fairly constant, and so we moved 200 yards to the south and camped, hoping that by the morning the movement would have ceased.

Above the noise of the primus stove we could not hear the noise of the pressuring ice, nor at first could we believe Fritz's shouts of alarm that the pressure ridge was now only 30 yards away and bearing down on us. The tent had suddenly become a tomb and the sleeve entrance our only chance of escape. We stuffed our gear into bags, heaved them outside and plunged out after them into the night. In the dim light of the aurora, the advancing pressure looked like an enormous breaking wave. Black sea was welling up from its base as though it was boiling, and we could feel dull shocks through the ice as the huge blocks of ice slid forward and thudded onto the floe, and with the noise growing louder and the outline of the ridge towering above us we loaded the sledges, hitched up the dogs and drove them in the only direction we could go—into the chaos of pressure hummocks to our south.

For a while all I could see ahead of me were the hurricane lanterns that were carried on the other three sledges; but the night was dead still—I could hear every sound and word crystal clear. I could sense the nearness of the pressure ridge behind me and smell the sea. I could hear it chewing up the small patch of smooth ice which had been our camp site only a few minutes ago. For the first and not the last time on that journey we looked deep into the throat of death, and for some unaccountable reason it rejected us.

The Long Haul

On the morning of 4 March, 12 hours after the ice had ceased moving, we drove our teams out onto the mush ice. By that time it was about three miles wide at its narrowest point and all it had needed was a five knot wind from any direction, or for the floes on either side to have shifted and the whole lot would have sighed and relaxed and the four of us would have sunk without trace through that icy 'porridge' to the icy sea beneath it. But after a few hours we got across and over the next three days we fought a losing battle against the drift of ice. What we gained by day we lost at night—and it was the nights which we most dreaded; those cold, black nights when we each took turns to plod wearily around the camp with a lantern, sniffing the air, listening for the slightest sound that might give our sleeping companions a few more minutes' or seconds' warning that the ice was breaking up and we must run to save our lives.

By the evening of 8 March we had drifted to within 17 miles (18 km) of Point Barrow and the sky to the south-west was ominous and black with the reflection of open water. By the morning of the 9th we could hear the sound of the waves lapping at our floe and in sheer desperation we made a few miles. But without then knowing it, our luck had turned, and when Providence allowed us to cross a lead that was half a mile wide and had a covering of only four inches of ice which bent under the weight of our sledges, we knew that we had won through.

Above: Once clear of the dangerous coastal currents we should now have been able to concentrate our efforts on making good progress across the pack ice in the chosen direction; but although old floes were becoming more numerous, and the action of the ice more predictable, we discovered that there was much more broken young ice than we had expected—in fact, probably as much as 70 per cent of the ice cover between latitudes 75° and 77°N was less than two feet thick, and much of it less than six inches.

Below: Our progress was also slowed down occasionally by areas where the floes were shattered and the whole vast area was in motion, slowly swirling, eddying— a confusion of currents, counter-currents, and winds which moved the sea ice like brittle scum in a stagnant pool stirred from below. Being by this time so far behind schedule, we had no alternative but to make what little progress we could by taking the line of least resistance in our efforts to go north.

Above and right: When the leads were too wide and at right angles to our course and when a short reconnaissance offered no hope of finding a point where the two floes touched we would convert a sledge into a boat and ferry the whole caravan across.

Below: But these 'boating' operations were time consuming, and time was what we lacked.

Arrival at Summer Camp

'At local noon on Midsummer's Day our latitude fix showed 81°18'N, an advance of only half a mile on our position of two days earlier. That position fix put us at the same distance from the Pole of Relative Inaccessibility as Shackleton was from the South Pole in 1908 at the time he and his companions turned back: 98 geographical miles (156 km).

I doubted then that we would get much further, for the old floes were badly split; black sea pools and leads were spreading like a stain and we were travelling on borrowed time.

'Our last seven days before setting up summer camp on 4 July at latitude 81°33'N, longitude 165°29'W were physically the hardest of the whole journey. We drove the dogs out of their depth in wet snow and melt-water pools, and had to drag them out one by one. We put two teams together and drove them through on extended traces with all four of us pushing, stumbling and shouting ourselves hoarse. The ice floes were by that time a shimmering maze of melt-water pools and leads. In places there were cracks every 15 yards. Each day the pools were deeper and the dogs more reluctant to plough their way through dragging a sledge. We were fighting a losing battle with the drift—a hopeless effort to travel north west in search of a safer area in which to sit out the summer melt. We had come a long way. Since leaving Barrow on 21 February we had sledged 1,180 route miles.

'We had sledged farther from land over the polar pack ice than any other explorers. We had measured floe thicknesses and snow densities almost every day. We had kept logs of wildlife, and logs on the types and ages of the ice across which we had travelled. We had recorded synoptic weather data which we had coded and then transmitted daily to Squadron Leader Freddy Church at Barrow, and he in turn had passed it on to the U.S. Weather Bureau and the British Meteorological Office. But sadly we had failed to travel far enough, for we were still in the influence of a current which occasionally took a shift to the east. We had, however, reached our physical limit and could do no more.'

Above and below: From the very moment the idea of crossing the Arctic Ocean had first occurred to me over four years before, I had always known that my two most difficult decisions would be the decision to stop and set up our summer camp, and the even more critical choice of a floe on which to establish our winter quarters for the five-month drift through the polar night, and by 3 July, with only 10 travelling days left before the Canadian Air Force would fly out the summer supply drop, our situation was desperate. The sledges were bogging down in deep slush and the ice across which we were travelling was too thin to survive the summer melt.

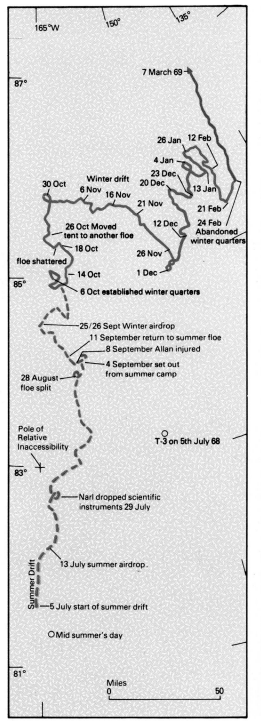

165°W 150° 135°

7 March 69

26 Jan 12 Feb
4 Jan
23 Dec
20 Dec 13 Jan
30 Oct Winter drift
6 Nov 16 Nov
21 Nov 21 Feb
26 Oct Moved 12 Dec 24 Feb
tent to another floe Abandoned
18 Oct winter quarters
floe shattered 26 Nov
14 Oct 1 Dec
6 Oct established winter quarters

25/26 Sept Winter airdrop
11 September return to summer floe
8 September Allan injured
28 August 4 September set out
floe split from summer camp

Pole of
Relative T-3 on 5th July 68
Inaccessibility

Narl dropped scientific
instruments 29 July

13 July summer airdrop
Summer Drift
5 July start of summer drift

Mid summer's day

87°
85°
83°
81°

Miles
0   50

But on that day providence presented us with an old floe, beyond which was another even larger one, and beyond it a giant floe which stretched to the horizon like a vast, dazzling ice sheet. We had seen no floes as big or as safe looking in the last 800 miles (1,030 km) of our journey— and by then we had neither the choice nor the desire to go a single mile farther.

Summer Drift

The luxury of not having physically to travel in order to make progress towards the Pole took a little while to get used to, for between the 5th and 9th of July the floe on which we had parked ourselves was blown 35 miles (56 km) due north. At an average of seven miles a day, this was more than our average since leaving Barrow—almost a full two miles a day more!

This wild weather, however, did not last, and as the wind died away, the speed of our northward drift decreased until at last it lost its novelty and merged with the awful monotony of the melting floes around us. During the whole month of July the absolute range of temperature was only 4°C (with a maximum of plus three) and often the temperature varied less than two degrees for periods of several days. It was misty, miserable, and very sticky— the relative humidity as often as not in the region of 90 per cent. We saw the sun through a screen of drizzle, and everything was limp and wet. The dogs lay around on the tops of the hummocks, panting and occasionally yawning with boredom and scratching off their moulting fur. They looked around the misty horizon expecting nothing, and seeing nothing went back to sleep.

There were times, nevertheless, when I envied them, for my commitments and my responsibilities left me little time for rest. Meanwhile the sticky mists closed in, squeezing and releasing us like some enormous spectral lung in which we were imprisoned, and the odours of decay and sodden fabric clung to us and to our camp like grease.

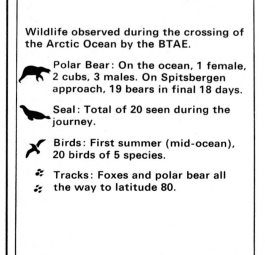

Wildlife observed during the crossing of the Arctic Ocean by the BTAE.

Polar Bear: On the ocean, 1 female, 2 cubs, 3 males. On Spitsbergen approach, 19 bears in final 18 days.

Seal: Total of 20 seen during the journey.

Birds: First summer (mid-ocean), 20 birds of 5 species.

Tracks: Foxes and polar bear all the way to latitude 80.

Left: At what range a polar bear can scent the odours of a camp there is no way of knowing, but on three occasions during the last week of July, when our floe was drifting within a few miles of the Pole of Inaccessibility, we were visited by hungry bears—all three of which reluctantly we were obliged to kill. The meat of course provided the dogs with a fresh and very acceptable change from their regular diet of pemmican, but since these were the first bears we had seen on the journey, and we had sighted only 12 ringed seals and 20 birds in the five months that we had been on the ice, it is clearly very fortunate that we had not trusted in Stefansson's theory and relied solely on hunting in order to survive.

Right: We had up to this point in the journey lost only three dogs and all three we had been glad to be rid of since for one reason or another they would have been a distracting element in the teams and would thereby have endangered the party. The remaining 37, however, were fit, strong and fairly compatible and as we could ill-afford to lose any more, a little surgery was sometimes required.

Below: We had been hoping to find a good number of seals out in the middle of the Arctic Ocean during the summer months, but only one was sighted. The reason for Dr Koerner's dives, however, was his professional interest in the ice and his need to get a seal's eye view of the underside of the floe on which we were drifting.

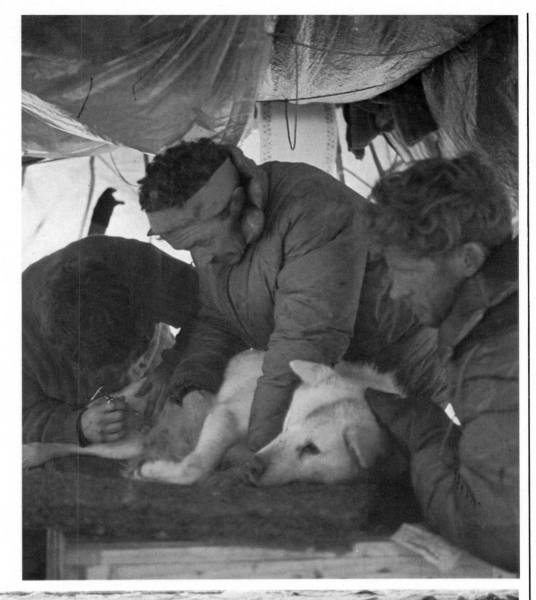

Navigation and Scientific Work

'Meltville' as the Press called it, was a hamlet of two polar pyramid tents and a marquee constructed from five of the 50 odd parachutes that had rained down on us on 13 July when the Canadian Forces delivered our summer supply drop. From the packing crates and boxes, we built ourselves tables and chairs, and for the first time since leaving Barrow we sat that night all together at table and ate our evening meal of stew in a moderately civilized manner. There was something of a party atmosphere that night in the bright and airy shelter—the first of many pleasant evenings the four of us spent together. During the day Allan used it as a place in which he could spread out his charts and do his computations.

Outside and only a few yards from the tent, the theodolite always sat firm on its tripod, levelled and ready for those rare occasions when the sun would burn a hole in the mist and Allan could measure its altitude. With a precise time fix for each observation, a nautical almanac and a set of tables, he could compute our position and record our current rate of drift, and this information always took priority over any other news that I transmitted once a day to Freddy Church at Barrow.

Of the four of us, Fritz was by far the busiest. First up every morning and last to bed at night, he worked for 17 hours a day. He seemed to be almost continually on the move across the floe from one delicate instrument to another, measuring the temperature profiles through the four metres of ice, and the minute changes in the wind, temperature and humidity in the air column five metres above the melting surface of the floe.

His work, he hoped, would give an insight into the total ice production of the Arctic Ocean at a time when its influence on world climate and glaciation was attracting the interest of many of the world's most respected polar scientists.

He had to know the mean thickness of the old floes and what percentage of the 5,000,000 square miles of the Arctic Ocean was covered by them. He had to know what proportion of the ocean was ice free at different stages in the year, and how much incoming radiation was absorbed and how much reflected by the many different ice forms. He had to know how the ice that was circulating differed from the ice of the trans-polar stream.

Some of these questions could be answered by aerial reconnaissance, submarines and the American and Russian scientific drifting stations; but there were many gaps in man's knowledge that could only be filled by a dedicated scientist who had the will and the courage to cross the Arctic Ocean on foot. Dr Fritz Koerner, like Nansen before him, had that vision and determination which his critics lacked.

Autumn Sledging

Our parachute tent by 4 September had become a grimy hovel. The ceiling was sagging with the weight of time and the place reeked with the odour of wet wood and stagnant water. Some of the floorboards were submerged; others, pedestalled on slippery ice, were wedged with cans and metal spikes and the moment had come to move on. In five weeks we would lose the sun and sink quickly into darkness. Already our shapeless shelter was casting long shadows across a scene that was no longer familiar, for by then the first snow of winter had settled on the squalor and puddles that pockmarked the surface around our camp and transformed an icescape, wet-green and rotten, into a dazzling wilderness.

But the floe on which we had spent the summer had served us well. In the 60 days we had been camped upon it, we had drifted almost two and a half degrees due north—an average of 2.7 miles a day. This was much more than we had expected or even hoped for, and we were now only 92 statute miles from the position where, in my original plan, I had calculated we would be at the end of the summer drift. Alas, that difference was mostly in longitude. We were too far east and would, if we were to stay at the summer floe, almost certainly change course sometime early in the winter and start drifting to the east in the influence of the currents that circulate in a clockwise gyral in that part of the Arctic Ocean.

We had to break away from the gyral and correct our course. We had to aim at reaching latitude 85°30'N, longitude 175°E by 20 September, and in that vicinity spend four days looking around for a nest of giant floes on which to set up our winter quarters. On 25 September the Canadian Forces would fly out our massive winter supply drop. If we were lucky enough to reach that position, a strong, steady and favourable winter's drift was assured, for we would be in the trans-polar drift stream and heading straight for the North Pole. But that position was 172 statute miles to our north west. To reach it in 15 days would mean averaging eleven and a half miles

a day over a surface more treacherous than any we had sledged across in the last six months.

At 1.40 pm we set off. But the melt pools that had 'burned' through the floes were now bottomless holes capped with a thin film of ice, which supported a soft blanket of freshly fallen snow. It was the same with the racks of razor-sharp crystals that carpeted the beds of the drained meltwater pools. Old cracks and fractures were now dangerously undercut, and the snow-covered pits of slush in places were knee deep.

It was into one of these hidden traps that Allan fell on the fourth day out. He had sprained his back the day before; but it was the second jarring shock to his spine which put a stop to our desperate struggle to find a way through the broken ice — and almost brought the Expedition itself to an untimely end.

The Winter Supply Drop

By the time we reached Allan it was obvious to all of us that he was in a bad way. In the short time that Ken had left him to call us back, Allan had seized up—he could no longer move his legs and seemed to be frozen into the position in which he fell. What made the situation worse was that Allan's body temperature was falling so rapidly that there was no time to move him to a safer place. We therefore had no choice but to set the tent up over him on a pan of ice surrounded by grinding pressure, which might split the small floe at any moment.

With the three of us concentrating on the one job, we soon had Allan sheltered and warmed up and the morphine in due course relieved his pain; but although Ken had already given us a warning of the seriousness of Allan's injury while we were putting up the tent, the news he gave us after examining Allan was shattering. Allan, in Ken's opinion, was in no fit state to continue the journey and should be sent out at the first opportunity.

. Distressing though this report was, it seemed to Fritz and I that there might be a way that Allan could stay with us—at least for the winter. But the first and very urgent need was to find a safer camp site, and so while Ken remained with Allan, Fritz and I set off to try and locate the summer floe. We were unable to return along our outward track, for in the four days since we left the summer floe the route had been smashed up behind us, but by taking a guess at its direction and a circuitous course we found it, and on the 11th, one week after leaving the summer floe, we returned to it with Allan strapped to the sledge on the upturned boat, which served very well as a stretcher. During the three days following our return, Fritz and I made a thorough reconnaissance of the area in which we had spent the summer. Things had changed considerably since we had first found that area of old floes—they were by this time badly broken up; but there were still a few suitable sites for the winter quarters, and on 25 September we received our winter supply drop from 435 Squadron of the Canadian Air Force.

The two C-130 Hercules, after having made their first low pass of our camp in close formation, had separated and taken up stations a few minutes apart and systematically peppered our chosen floe with 70 parachute loads of supplies for men and dogs totalling 28 tons—and the only loss was a dozen bottles of H.P. Sauce!

The setback, both for Allan and for the Expedition, had been a terrible blow; but luck had not been entirely against us, for by the time we returned to the summer floe it was about 16 miles farther north than when we had left it, and the favourable drift continued right through to 6 October—the date on which officially we established our winter quarters. On that date our floe crossed the 85th parallel at longitude 162°W—which meant that in the month since leaving the summer floe we had been carried by the drift one degree due north. But our luck, and Allan's was about to change.

Winter Quarters

After a three-day wait at the drifting station T-3 for the weather to improve, an attempt to reach us in a Twin-Otter and evacuate Allan was called off, and Allan, who had not wanted to be evacuated anyway, breathed a great sigh of relief. But a hut on drifting pack ice is not the best place to recuperate from an injury as we were very soon reminded, for on the morning of 20 October, only two weeks after we had erected the hut, the floe disintegrated.

Within a few minutes the fractures had opened into 'smoking' leads—one of them only a few feet from a team of dogs and 70 yards from the hut. By that time, however, the long polar night had already closed in, and finding an alternative site for the hut in that pitch black, groaning wilderness seemed such a daunting and hopeless task that we were tempted to stay where we were. There was, after all, a slight chance that our shattered floe would settle down and 'heal' itself in due course—we even found ourselves arguing that it was perhaps a good omen that none of our depots had been lost; but by the next morning, after a sleepless night, we knew we had to move.

Eventually, after about two hours of fumbling around in the dark, Fritz and I found ourselves on what seemed to be a sizeable floe about two miles to the north east of the hut. There we separated and sledged

parallel to each other about 200 yards apart. On each sledge we carried a hurricane lantern and our general heading we kept in check with the luminous aircraft compasses that were mounted between the handlebars; thus by keeping a mental log of the number of times the light of the other sledge disappeared and the duration of each obstruction, we were able to judge by time and pace not only the size of each floe we crossed, but also, to a certain extent, the surface configuration. The need for some point of reference was of course vital. We had therefore left at the hut and on top of the strategic hummocks along our outward track three pressure lanterns on which occasionally we took compass bearings in order to plot our route,

and by this technique we found, in pitch darkness, a floe about twice as big as the one on which we had set up our hut.

The stores, having a higher priority than the hut, had to be moved first, and in temperatures of −30°F (−34°C) and below we spent the next five days relaying 27 tons of gear. Finally, on 26 October, we started dismantling the hut and shifting it section by section over the polished highway which now marked the route between the two sites, and the following morning came the turn of the items which had the lowest priority of all—our furniture.

A stranger sight I have never seen than those four sledges rattling through the night, their hurricane lamps casting weird light on an even

more weird cargo of desks, shelves, beds, tables, stove and stove-pipes. We were like the victims of some terrible earthquake, or the refugees from a battle-torn village, our crude furniture symbolic of man's struggle for survival. But like refugees we could not help wondering how many times during the next few months we would be obliged to move on with our sledge loads of furniture, stove and stove-pipes, always escaping into darkness, always the same skeletal rattle, the same pathetic junk worth more to its owner than its weight in gold.

The Long Polar Night

Late into the night of the 27th we worked erecting our hut on a square of fresh-water ice from which the snow had been cut, and in a wind which raised the weals of a whiplash on our faces, we worked all the following day outside securing the guy wires and sorting out the massive pile of gear that had been dumped nearby. Our position was then latitude 85°34'N, longitude 164°18'W; our winter quarters was re-established, but the muffled booms and pistol shots transmitted through the ice as it contracted with the cold had never seemed more ominous or our camp more vulnerable.

We probably lost about a month's work in our scientific programme as a result of that move, for although the move itself was carried out quicker than we had expected, it took us far longer in the darkness to sort out our gear and reorganize our depots, each one of which had to have a balanced selection of all the essential items of gear and an even distribution of food and fuel just in case in the event of a break-up of the floe, only one of our five depots survived. But once these hard physical chores had been done we got down to our programme of scientific work with the eagerness of a late arrival at a feast.

Allan was responsible for the geophysics, the generators and the navigation. Ken's programme was a comparative study of wool and synthetic fibres. My own work, as in the summer, was mostly concerned with the planning of the journey as a whole and the many contingency plans which might be needed should we fail to catch up on our original schedule. But it was Fritz who, as in the summer, seemed to work the hardest. His programme was an extension of his summer one, and from a scientific point of view, of course, his programme was greatly strengthened by the fact that he was able to conduct it in the same general ice location. He was able for instance to measure the growth rate of the ice at the same points at which in the summer he had measured the rate of melt, and from his daily tours of the floes in our vicinity he was able to report on any changes—and many changes there were.

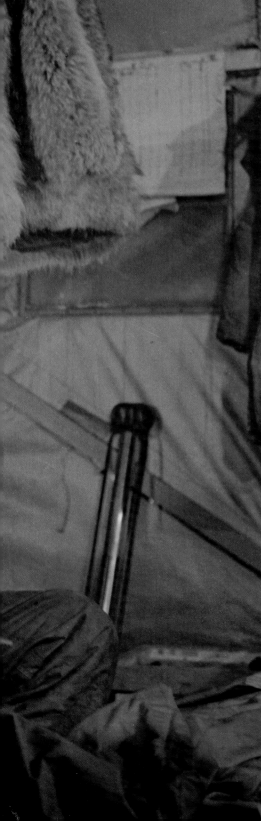

One of these, and perhaps the most significant, occurred at 1900 hrs GMT on 1 November. It entered Fritz's meteorological log as a breeze of 4 knots from the south-west. I also noticed it that day while I was driving my dog team back along the tracks to the site of our first winter quarters, but it did not occur to me at that time that the breeze I felt signalled the start of our drift to the east. We were at that time at latitude 85°48'N. We were to get no more help from the drift; but it had served us well—in the last four months it had been consistent almost to the point of being monotonous as it steadily closed on the Pole at a rate of two and a half miles a day.

From then on for the next four months, every night I would lie in my bed gazing up at the chart of the Arctic Ocean that was pasted on a board hung from the sloping ceiling of our hut and fret over the adverse drift that was robbing us of the bonus miles I had planned on collecting. Now we were drifting south-east, sometimes even south, and we were helpless.

Drifing Off Course

For the rest of the winter the ice around us incessantly creaked and groaned. There were times in our hut when even the roar of the three primuses and four pressure lamps could not drown the crunching, creaking sounds of the pressuring ice. By Christmas, however, we had grown so accustomed to these sounds that they no longer disturbed us—we had in any case too many other things to occupy our minds, for we were by then 350 miles (560 km) behind schedule and only half-way to our destination. The journey ahead seemed formidable. To reach Spitsbergen, we would have to travel as far in 100 days as the distance we had so far taken ten months to cover. To stand any chance, we would not only need a fair measure of luck, but we would have to work hard to deserve it.

Over the next few weeks, while the floes around us worked against each other and ate away the platform on which our hut lay purring with the noise of petrol engines, we each took our turn in the snow house assembling our heavy new sledges. It was a period that I now remember with nostalgia—that snowblock workshop with its tarpaulin roof and its false ceiling of parachutes held

up with skis; its sledge like some strange creature growing in a glistening womb above the vortices of warmth that rose from the primus stoves on the floor and those fine plumes of drift snow that formed great snow warts on the walls. I remember those days wrapped up in fur, hands gloved in white evening-dress silk, in that cold snow room where the breath vapour hung in a swirling cloud, 20°F (− 7°C) the temperature was; but outside it was −50°F (−45°C), and the ground drift was slithering like snakes across the floe and licking the walls of the shelter.

But by the beginning of January we were beginning once again to feel very vulnerable. In the light of the moon, we noticed what appeared to be water sky to our east and north-east and on investigating we found that the floes had relaxed and drifted apart—exposing a vast expanse of open water that stretched

to the horizon. Our hut was now only 50 yards from the edge of the floe in one direction and less than half a mile from the open sea at its greatest distance. For a whole month we lived in constant expectation that the floe at any moment would disintegrate, and so it came as something of a relief when at 4 am on 4 February it finally split in two. But our long drift mercifully was coming to an end—we had only three weeks left in which to suffer the frustrations of our southward drift, and three weeks to wait for the moon to return and give us some light to see our way.

By 23 February there was a hard-packed route winding five miles towards the retreating gloom on the northern horizon—a blazed trail that crossed the crests and troughs of the hummocked ice floes and swept gracefully over frozen lakes to the chaos of ice beyond. We were almost ready to leave that hut, to break free from that protective shell which had suddenly become a prison. Every instinct by then was straining for freedom, every fibre tense, every dog harnessed, every sledge ready to receive its load.

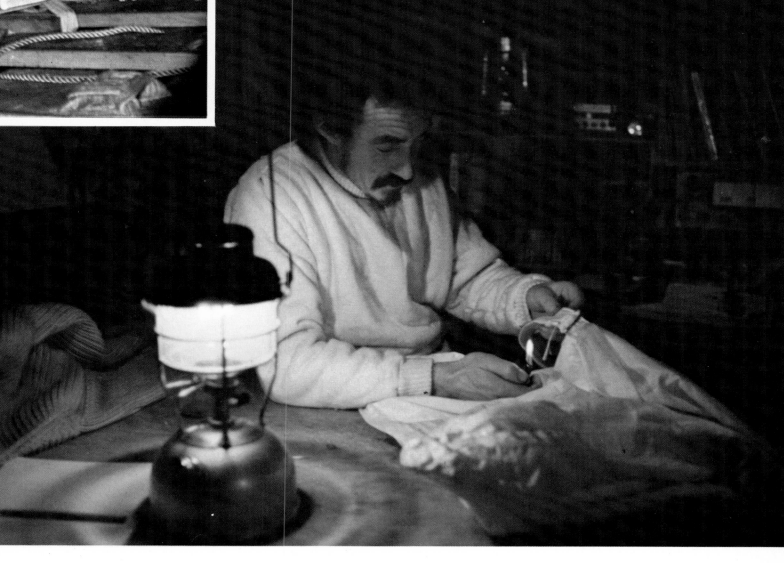

Abandon Ship!

It was six o'clock on the morning of 24 February 1969. I had already been awake for an hour or so, thinking about the journey ahead. The hut was in a shambles with half-sorted gear and was very cold, but within five minutes of Fritz lighting the lamp and the primus stove, the place had warmed up sufficiently for the rest of us to crawl out of our sleeping bags and roll them up. In fact, shambles apart, it was not unlike any other early start—until we were about halfway through breakfast, when suddenly a whole salvo of twangs vibrated through the hut.

Immediately all four of us made a dive for the door and tumbling outside found, as we had all expected, that the floe was splitting and opening all around us. One crack was only about 12 feet from the hut, and had it not changed direction about 20 yards away would have gone straight beneath us and dropped the whole hut into the cold, black sea. There was no time to go back into the hut to change into warmer gear and even though the temperature was minus forty and there was a stiff breeze blowing, we scrambled up the snow bank and scattered. The floe had cracked up like an eggshell and the whole area was opening up at a rate of several feet a minute. There was time only to rescue Fritz's dogs—mine and Allan's were cut off but safe. Ken's sledge and dogs by good fortune were on the same piece of ice as the hut, but within less than a quarter of an hour the pan of ice on which we were all reunited was separated from those on which the rest of our gear and dogs were marooned by a lead almost 50 feet wide.

Meanwhile the floes had started to gyrate, and with pressure building up in some places where the floes were touching and opening in others, what we now feared was that the pressure might set off a series of cracks at right angles which might run beneath the hut. We were now all four of us frozen to the core, and slithering back into the hut we literally stuffed everything that might be of any use whatsoever into bags and boxes and hurled them outside.

Fortunately the sledges were all safe (bottom) and having been partly loaded a few days before were quickly made ready. We sledged north towards the darkest quarter of the sky (left) with only Venus as a guide—a wilderness in monochrome through which the sledges weaved and rattled along a trail already blazed, and by the time we camped we had travelled the first five miles of the 1,700-mile (2,735-km) journey that lay ahead.

At the time of abandoning our winter quarters we were 322 statute miles from the Pole, and with only about four hours of twilight, we made very little progress for the first few days. The first real crisis, happened when on the third day out one of Allan's sledge runners split—a few days later mine did the same, and repairing them (right) was a long and miserable job.

The Pole

Below: By 9 March the relentless struggle was beginning to leave its mark on all of us, for by then we were travelling ten hours every day in temperatures down to −50°F (−45°C) and sometimes even lower. At times there seemed no end to the misery — no hope of ever reaching the Pole, no hope at times of continuing, or even of surviving.

Above right: But at our lowest ebb the sun returned. For the first time in five long months of night that beautiful, pulsating, living thing seemed slowly to explode itself out of the sea and renew in us what we had lost — our hope and energy.

Below: Then once again the mists rolled in, and thickening as we neared the Pole, the sun shone through them without warmth or light enough to cast a shadow. Day and night now fused together.

I sent only three other messages on that occasion: one to our patron, HRH the Duke of Edinburgh, one to the chairman of our committee, and one to the editor of *The Sunday Times* our sponsoring newspaper — but alas they were all premature!

As the message said — the Pole had been reached according to our dead reckoning. We had not seen the sun for several days, and had it remained hidden for a few more hours we would have been on our way to Spitsbergen none the wiser that we had not in fact reached the Pole but had passed it at a distance of about seven miles. But with the sun's untimely reappearance a few minutes after I had sent the message, we realised our error, and with 15 hours left in which to reach the North Pole before the date changed to 6 April, we set off in good spirits.

'I have the honour to inform Your Majesty that today, April fifth, at 0700 hrs Greenwich Mean Time, the British Trans-Arctic Expedition by dead reckoning reached the North Pole 407 days after setting out from Point Barrow, Alaska. My companions of the crossing party, Allan Gill, Major Kenneth Hedges, RAMC, and Dr Roy Koerner, together with Squadron-Leader Church, RAF, our radio relay officer at Point Barrow, are in good health and spirits and hopeful that by forced marches and a measure of good fortune the Expedition will reach Longyearbyen, Spitsbergen by Midsummer's Day of this year, thus concluding in the name of our country the first surface crossing of the Arctic Ocean
(W. W. Herbert, Expedition Leader).'

But it was an elusive spot to find and fix—that place where two sets of meridians meet and all directions are south. Trying to set foot upon it was like trying to step on the shadow of a bird that is hovering overhead, for the surface across which we were moving was itself a moving surface on a planet that was spinning about an axis beneath our feet. Even our final fix which showed that we had crossed the Pole about one mile back along our tracks at about 2 am on 6 April, was only a record of where we had been at the time of the observation, for by the time we awoke the following morning, we had drifted back across the Pole and it lay north in a different direction.

Longitude 30° East

For the first time in almost 14 months we were intentionally heading south. We had the feeling we were heading for home at last, and not without good reason, for we were heading straight down the Greenwich meridian—and from the Pole you can't aim more precisely for the capital of England than that.

To have continued along that meridian, however, would have been both pointless and rash, for the only sensible approach to Spitsbergen, should you ever be tempted to do so by sledge, is on a south-west track—to close on land, in other words, *with* the drift of ice. And so for this reason we changed our course and moved over to longitude 30°E and the dreaded forced march routine. For 15 hours a day we travelled in a desperate bid to reach Spitsbergen before the break-up of the ice; but there were many times in this final stage of the trans-Arctic trek when we came within a hair's breadth of losing the one thing that we still had in our favour—the element of luck.

The 26 April is a case in point: I had left my dogs and gone forward to give Allan a hand in getting his team across a smashed-up and groaning strip of ice, and no sooner had I joined him when the mush ice all around us started to slacken and 'boil'. The pan of ice on which we were standing suddenly reared up and started sliding towards the churning ice. Instinctively Allan cut his dogs free and scrambled to the far bank while I slithered back across the heaving ice in an effort to save my own team and sledge. The whole area was cracking up— Fritz and Ken were caught in it as well and it was some time before we were able to get our three teams to a slightly safer place.

Allan meanwhile had discovered that he was cut off from the floe beyond by a fissure in the ice about 14 feet deep, and the mush ice separating us was now in a highly dangerous state. Several times I was about to make a dash across it when it would suddenly boil up, and green blocks, the size of bungalows, would rise out of the stew of ice debris and collapse with a dull thud back into the mush. I was reminded of the stories I had been told by the Eskimos in Barrow, who had seen a whole party of hunters caught on such ice when it had relaxed, and their descriptions of the sight and sounds of that ice as it loosened and sucked their companions down, crushed them, and threw up the pulverized bodies amongst the stew of blood-soaked mush.

Not until it had quietened could I possibly get across, but even when I did the danger had not passed: we had to lower the sledge into the fissure, at the bottom of which was a 'floor' of compacted slush so weak in places that we broke through it several times. Had the walls of that fissure suddenly closed, or parted only five or six inches as we were hauling the sledge through that trap, we would have met our end right there. Such was our dependence at times on the element of luck.

7 April 1969—from Buckingham Palace: 'I send my warmest congratulations to you and the other members of The British Trans-Arctic Expedition on reaching the North Pole. My husband and I are delighted that you are well and wish you the best of luck for the rest of your journey. Elizabeth R.'

7 April 1969—from No. 10 Downing Street: 'Yours is a feat of endurance and courage which ranks with any in polar history. My colleagues and I send you our heartfelt congratulations and our best wishes for a safe and triumphant completion of your journey. Harold Wilson.'

Landfall

By 20 May the ice was slushy and for the first time since the summer of 1968 we could smell the sea. Wildlife suddenly became abundant, perhaps because of an upwelling of water near the edge of the continental shelf, or perhaps we were on the southern dispersal edge of the ice pack—we did not really know; but all this wildlife intensified the excitement we were now beginning to feel, for with a good day's travel on 23 May by my calculations we ought to sight land—15 months to the day after losing sight of Point Barrow on the other side of the Arctic Ocean.

Several times that day we searched the horizon, but without reward. At 10.50 pm however, I noticed a large hummock past which the other three sledges had swept without stopping and climbing this hummock I stuck a harpoon into its summit, steadied my rifle against it and took aim at the cloud base directly ahead. Through the telescopic sight I suddenly saw land—it was climbing out of the horizon into the cloud rolls; a grey-and-white wall of land, hazy with distance, hostile-looking, bleak and spanning several degrees. I lowered

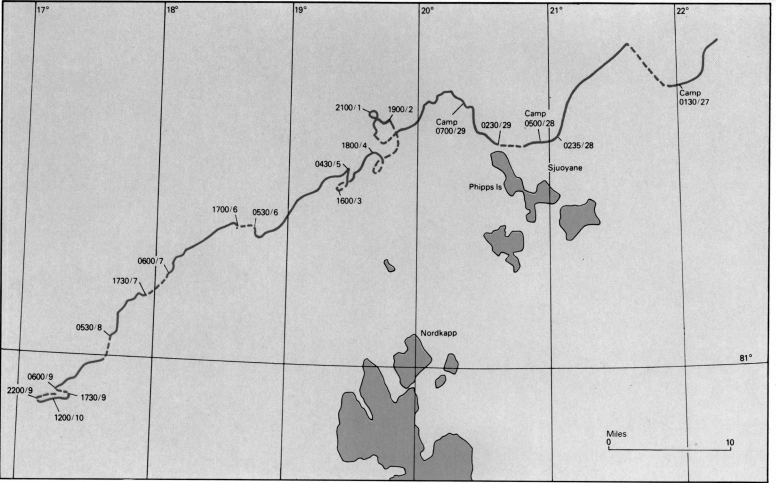

'Herbert to Church—A.1080: Land sighted directly ahead 2055 GMT 459 days out from Barrow. Present position 81°18'N, 22°00'E— 29 nautical miles NNE of Phipps Island.'

my aim very slightly to the pack ice— now I could see all three sledges in line ahead, widely separated but dead on course. My message to Freddy Church that night had the ring of jubilation:

During the next four days, however, not only were we constantly harassed by bears as we waded through slush and melt water up to our shins and hacked our way through some of the most chaotic ice we had ever seen, but it was becoming depressingly obvious that our chances of making a landing were decreasing by the hour and that the last few miles were going to be the most uncomfortable and probably the most hazardous few miles of the entire journey.

The one and only hope of getting onto Phipps Island was to cross a belt of mush ice to one of the small ice pans that was drifting with it. But within a few hundred yards the risk we were taking seemed suicidal, for the whole floating mass of ice rubble was shimmering and heaving like some vast cauldron of stew. Not once in 15 months had we camped on a smaller or faster moving pan of ice than we did on 28 May. For 22 hours we were without any possible route of escape and drifting on a collision course for the northern tip of the island.

What saved us was that the floes to our north were constricted in their westward drift between Phipps Island and a tiny rocky island about two and a half miles to the NNW, and when those floes moved in and compressed the mush ice it gave us those few vital seconds we needed to scramble across to the safer ice beyond. Now our last chance of reaching land was that rugged island, but there too any hope of getting ashore at first seemed impossible— and so we set up our camp about a mile from the island and over the radio I sent out a message to HMS *Endurance* advising Captain Peter Buchanan that we had abandoned all hope of reaching land and would now head straight for the ship which at that time was held fast in the ice about 120 miles (192 km) to our south-west.

57

Journey's End

When we awoke the following morning we found to our surprise that an eddy had held the mush ice in tightly to that small rocky island and we had one last chance of getting across. It was, however, too great a risk for all four of us to make the attempt for the floes needed only to slacken a few feet and we might all four of us have been cut off from our sledges—it was essential therefore that one man stayed at camp, and while a second man kept a watchful eye on the ice about half way across the mush ice belt, the other two would make their bid to reach the rock.

It proved a wise precaution, for as Allan and Ken were returning from their successful landing on the island I noticed that the ice was beginning to slacken off, and no sooner had all three of us reached the floe when that three-quarters of a mile of mush ice opened into a sea of slush and slimy ice not one piece of which was big enough to support the weight of a man.

But it was a few moments before the full significance of what Allan and Ken had done got through to me, and when it did it was not through any critical assessment, but simply in the tangible evidence of a chunk of rock which Ken thoughtfully, but without ceremony, pressed into

'At 1900 hrs GMT 29 May, a landing was made by Allan Gill and Major Ken Hedges RAMC on a small rocky island at latitude 80°49'N, longitude 20°23'E, after a scramble across three-quarters of a mile of mush ice and gyrating ice pans. This landing, though brief, concluded the first surface crossing of the Arcti Ocean—a journey of 3,620 route mile from Point Barrow, Alaska, via the Nort Pole. The four members of the crossin party on their 464th day on drifting ic are now heading across broken ice pac towards a rendezvous with HM Endurance.'

my hand.

I went into the tent and waited for that heady moment of triumph to pass before drafting out my message for Freddy Church to pass to London (above right).

In the 15 months we had been on the Arctic Ocean we had grown accustomed to the sounds and the sight of the drifting ice, and had developed habits of survival which required no conscious thought. The adventure was no longer the novel

situation, but the journey as a whole; and its climax not the sight of land but the sight from land of the ice across which we had come. I had for several days sensed this distance on my back, sensed the tiredness of all those miles in my limbs, the longing for land and the release of my burden—that total commitment to success, without which six years of my life would have been wasted.

But although in the historical sense the journey was done, we still had to reach the ship, which by that time was about 105 miles (168 km) to our south west. By the thirtieth we were in range of the helicopters, but at that range they would only be able to take out the men—the dogs, sledges, and all our scientific records and instruments would have to be left on the ice. We naturally chose to go on; but each day the struggle became harder, the polar bears more troublesome and the ice more dangerous. Finally, when we had reduced the gap between us and the ship to 40 miles (64 km) and were in range for a helicopter evacuation from the ice with all our gear and our dogs, we called an end to our struggle, and our epic journey of 3,720 route miles (5952 km) finally was ended.

And of what value was this journey? It is as well for those who ask such a question that there are others who feel the answer and never need to ask.

Acknowledgements

Wally Herbert: Pages 6, 7 top left and
right, 11 bottom right, 12–15,
19 bottom, 22 bottom, 23 bottom,
24 top and centre, 26–8, 29 top and
bottom left, 30–37, 38 bottom, 39–57,
58 top, 59

The Sunday Times: Pages 7 bottom,
16–17, 21–22 top, 23 top, 24 bottom,
25, 27 inset, 29 centre right and
bottom right, 38 top, 58 bottom,
59 inset

Hamlyn Group: Page 8 top centre
Frank Herrmann: Pages 18, 19 top, 20
John Topham Picture Library: Pages
11 top right, 8 bottom centre
Library of Congress: Page 11 top left
Tom Lovell: Page 10
The Mansell Collection: Pages 8
bottom left, 9 bottom
National Maritime Museum:
Page 8 top
Paul Popper Ltd: Page 9 centre
Radio Times Hulton Picture Library:
Page 9 top right
The Royal Geographical Society:
Page 8 bottom
Thomson Newspapers Ltd: Page 57

Index